Original title:
The Porch That Feels Like Home

Copyright © 2025 Creative Arts Management OÜ
All rights reserved.

Author: Lila Davenport
ISBN HARDBACK: 978-1-80587-155-2
ISBN PAPERBACK: 978-1-80587-625-0

Cozy Cliffnotes of Life

Gathered 'round with snacks galore,
We share our tales, and giggle more.
The cat jumps high, but lands with grace,
While I still search for my lost keys' place.

Witty jabs with half-filled cups,
As deep discussions dive like pups.
Chasing dreams that run so fast,
Yet spilling drinks? That's a blast!

Warmth Held in Each Gaze

Our eyes spark joy without a sound,
Like secret jokes that spin around.
The moonlight spills, it plays just right,
As laughter dances through the night.

With comfy chairs, we plot and scheme,
About the dinner that turned to cream.
Oh, the way we recount a fall,
And find humor in it all!

Companionable Silence of the Evening

In pauses hang the best of times,
Like silly gifs or cheesy rhymes.
Bookmarks left in laughter's book,
As crickets join, the night they took.

A gentle breeze brings tales of old,
Of doggie fails and sibling gold.
Where silence speaks in chuckles bright,
And warms us up, throughout the night.

Breaths Between Words

Pauses filled with coffee's steam,
As we plot the most outrageous dream.
In between the quips and puns,
The heartbeats count like playful runs.

We share our quirks, our funny quirks,
From cooking fails to blender jerks.
In every breath, a memory stirs,
As we laugh off life's little blurs.

Lattes and Long Talks

Sipping coffee, oh so hot,
We spill secrets, laugh a lot.
Every sip brings giggles, cheers,
Our dreams, our hopes—fueled by beers.

Caffeine buzz and witty jests,
With silly hats, we're truly blessed.
In our world, no cares persist,
The barista's eye-roll? A twist!

Underneath the Vast Starlit Canopy

Stars wink down, they know our jokes,
We giggle at the moon's fine pokes.
In the night, the critters chime,
Each sound provides a punchline prime.

A raccoon stares, as if to say,
'Is this my stage? I want my pay!'
We laugh until the sun breaks light,
Our antics painting skies so bright!

A Haven of Sweet Reminiscence

Old stories flow like sweet warm tea,
With each tale, we laugh with glee.
Remember when the cat wore pants?
We fell off chairs in wild, wild chants!

With snacks piled high on silly plates,
We reenact our younger dates.
Each memory, a priceless gem,
In this silly tale, we're living stem!

Whims of the Night Air

Fireflies dance, a light parade,
As we scheme the plans we've laid.
Crickets join in—who knew they sang?
A full-on concert, our hearts clang!

With goofy hats, the night's a riot,
Who needs elegance? We just fly it.
Spilling laughs into the warm breeze,
These carefree moments—oh, what a tease!

Hearth of Heartfelt Moments

Where the sun spills its rays,
With a drink that's a tease,
We laugh at our own jokes,
And chase off the bees.

The chair squeaks a tune,
As we tell tales of old,
In comfy old slippers,
And stories retold.

A cat on the ledge,
Prowls for a bite,
While snacks make their rounds,
In the warm summer night.

We toast to the chaos,
Of life's silly game,
With each clink of glasses,
We're all just the same.

Haven of Solace and Serenity

The coffee pot bubbles,
Like dreams in a stew,
While kids chase the dog,
In a wild game of 'who?'

The wind chimes are laughing,
With every slight breeze,
As squirrels scurry by,
To steal all our cheese.

We gossip and giggle,
At the neighbor's odd ways,
While counting the minutes,
'Fore the end of our days.

With each funny quirk,
Life's moments we share,
Our hearts turn to homies,
No place can compare.

Railing Wrapped in Dreams

The railing tells secrets,
Of dreams that we shared,
Like midnight ice cream,
When no one really cared.

We built silly castles,
In the air, not the sand,
While the wind made requests,
To play in our band.

Our feet, propped up high,
On the rails worn with time,
We crack up with joy,
At the world's silly rhyme.

With every snickering laugh,
And the playful exchange,
We find life's little joys,
As the laughter will range.

Echoes of Laughter and Love

The echoes of giggles,
We can't seem to stop,
As we tiptoe on jokes,
And dance with a mop.

The shadows are grinning,
As the sun starts to fade,
While we sip on our drinks,
In the fun that we've made.

Each tick of the clock,
Makes our memories bloom,
In the warmth of the night,
We make our own room.

With every soft chuckle,
And silly parade,
We find ours is a place,
Where the laughter won't fade.

Refuge in Fading Light

At dusk, the cat's the boss,
Ignoring my soft pleas,
I sip my tea with sass,
She naps upon my knees.

The neighbors are quite odd,
Talking to their fence,
I chuckle at the scene,
The twilight's full pretense.

An owl hoots, I raise a brow,
Is that a bird or a ghost?
The shadows play their games,
And I just laugh the most.

With crickets as my band,
I dance in my own way,
In fading light, I'm home,
Nothing's here to sway.

Memories Nestled in Wood

Wooden chair squeaks like me,
As I munch on chips of cheese,
My thoughts, a playful spree,
While squirrels plot with ease.

That wooden swing's seen it all,
From whispers to loud bites,
It sways with a gentle call,
Under the watch of night lights.

Grandpa's stories linger near,
As fireflies take their flight,
He claimed he caught a deer,
But I think it was slight!

In this cozy nook I find,
A haven, sweet and kind,
Each laugh, a memory shared,
As starlight's gently bared.

Shelter of Solitude and Stories

My favorite chair is grand,
With mismatched stripes galore,
It swallows me like sand,
While tales tumble and roar.

A mug of cocoa spills,
As laughter fills the air,
The neighbor's dog now shrills,
In a most awkward stare.

The wind begins to howl,
Just as I start to read,
A ghostly tale, a growl,
Of haunted, daring deed.

I chuckle at my fate,
With shadows keeping score,
A book, a friend, I wait,
For more fun tales galore.

Corner of Quiet Comfort

In the corner, sipping slow,
With chocolate crumbs in hand,
I hear a wild rooster crow,
Thinking he's in a band.

The hammock sways, a gentle tease,
As squirrels play their tricks,
I laugh, and with a breeze,
They stash away their picks.

Old shoes line the floor,
A collection of my past,
Each one tells a lore,
Of adventures built to last.

As dusk wraps up the day,
I sit here, sweetly still,
In this corner, I'll stay,
Where laughter's always chill.

Sunlight Dancing on Planks

Sunlight prances, right on cue,
It tickles toes and teases too.
A squirrel slides down, a little thief,
While I sip tea, trying to be brief.

The shadows play a game of hide,
With beams of joy dancing wide.
A neighbor's laughter spills like wine,
I can't help but chuckle, feeling fine.

Where Time Slows its Pace

Clock hands melt like butter's bliss,
In a moment's pause, I find my kiss.
The cat sprawls out, a sprawled-out king,
While I muse on life and the joy it can bring.

A bird hops in, it's quite the sight,
Worms are dancing, what a delight!
I raise my cup to the setting sun,
A toast to time, just having fun.

An Invitation to Stillness

Come sit a while, drop all your haste,
Mosquitoes take a break, no need for a chase.
The breeze whispers secrets, soft and light,
While I try not to doze off, holding tight.

A frog jumps by, croaking its song,
Reminds me how I've been all wrong.
Not rushing through life, oh what a treat,
Instead just lounging, feeling the heat.

Reflections on Weathered Wood

This old chair creaks, a trusty friend,
It knows my stories, it knows my bends.
The paint peels off like my best ideas,
But the laughter lingers, like forgotten cheers.

A raccoon waves, wearing its mask,
Stealing snacks, oh what a task!
We share a moment, under the sky,
It's just too funny, oh my, oh my!

Lanterns Lighting the Path

Twinkling lights hang off the eaves,
They guide the lost with wobbly leaves.
Mismatched chairs, a quirky sight,
Who needs a bar when you've got this light?

A cat jumps high, he thinks he's cool,
Wobbling around like a drunken fool.
Sipping lemonade, laughing loud,
As insects dance, we feel quite proud.

Flavors of Time in the Air

Peach pie cools on the table edge,
While Aunt Sue swears she'll make a pledge.
But later, she's caught with crumbs on her face,
We laugh so hard, we just can't race.

The kids are running with sticky hands,
Chasing fireflies in their make-believe lands.
One yells, "Caution!" but steps on a bug,
And suddenly, they all shout with a shrug.

Comfort Cradled in the Rafters

Hammocks swing with a gentle creak,
As grandpa dozes, snoring weak.
The ceiling fan spins tales from the past,
Making memories that are sure to last.

Old shoes pile high in the corner wide,
Each pair a story, a former pride.
We squabble over who'll clean the mess,
And laugh through chaos in our big old dress.

Swaying in the Embrace of Breeze

Wind whispers secrets between the leaves,
Like gossiping friends, it pauses, weaves.
A squirrel steals snacks like it's on a quest,
Meanwhile, we just sit back and jest.

A storm rolls in, the sky's turned gray,
But inside, we'll take it, come what may.
With popcorn flying, the laughter erupts,
In this place of joy, our hearts are filled up.

A Lifetime of Shadows

In the corner sits a cat,
Pretending it's a lion's throne.
Sipping tea from a broken mug,
Wish it could just use a phone.

Old chairs creak like ancient tales,
Telling secrets of the night.
A ghost in flip-flops strolls by,
Lighting up the dull twilight.

Laughter dances on the breeze,
Chasing fireflies like a game.
Who knew the breeze could giggle?
Even shadows seem to claim fame.

Wooden Slats and Memories

With every step, a squeaky laugh,
The floorboards make their snarky jokes.
A picnic basket filled with snacks,
That never really feeds the folks.

Rocking chairs defy all sense,
As we argue if they should sway.
The dog thinks he's a watchdog here,
But snoozes through the whole buffet.

Elders tell tales of yesteryears,
While kids throw crumbs in the air.
The butterflies just roll their eyes,
Not gifted in this "so-called" flair.

Crickets' Serenade at Dusk

Crickets tune their fiddles loud,
Twirling as they jump and play.
Fireflies are the disco lights,
No one knows they went astray.

The night's a stage for silly acts,
With raccoons playing hide and seek.
A squirrel joins the chaos dance,
Barking orders like a freak.

Laughter echoes with each chirp,
As frogs croak lines from old revue.
Who needs a fancy concert hall?
Nature's got the best debut.

Stories Woven in the Air

Whispers float on cotton clouds,
As kids share tales of daring feats.
A game of truth in wild guise,
While adults play sip-and-eat.

Tangled yarn of laughter rolls,
As spiders spin their webs anew.
Weaving tales with silly knots,
The kind that only best friends knew.

Dandelions boast in the breeze,
While ants march in perfect line.
Frolicsome stories linger here,
Like sunshine stuck in a vine.

Heartstrings of the Hearth

Sitting on my rickety chair,
The neighbor's dog gives me a stare.
I sip my tea, it tastes like grass,
I think my cat just let one pass.

The sun has set, but lights are bright,
I swear I saw a ghost take flight.
It's just the wind, or so I say,
That spooked the kids who came to play.

With each loud creak, the house calms down,
My slippers squeak—it's quite a sound.
A knock, a clatter, what's that noise?
My friends arrive—oh, it's just the boys!

By midnight, laughter fills the air,
We share old jokes and tales to spare.
The fire pit crackles, sparks take wing,
Who knew that toast could make us sing?

The Comfort of Open Spaces

Under the stars, we play charades,
A cat walks by, and I'm afraid.
My cousin trips, she spills her drink,
It's just a laugh, we hardly think.

The breeze comes in with a whoosh and sway,
It tickles us, and we shout hooray!
I throw a snack, and it flies wide,
The raccoons feast while we just bide.

The moonlight glimmers on the grass,
We dance like fools, it's quite a class.
Then someone yells, 'What's that behind?'
Just a shadow—oh, never mind!

As night grows deep, the stories flow,
Each one better, like fine dough.
With giggles loud and smiles all round,
In this wild space, pure joy is found!

Chasing Fireflies at Twilight

As dusk descends, we run outside,
With jars in hand and eyes so wide.
The flickers dance, a glowing show,
I trip on roots—oh no, oh no!

My friends all laugh, they think it's fun,
As I pretend I'm on the run.
One firefly gives me a bright stare,
Deciding if it should dare me there.

We capture glow with childish glee,
But one escapes and flies to me.
It lands upon my friend's warm nose,
And suddenly, a giggle grows.

The night is full of magic's light,
With every twinkle, pure delight.
So here we are, in laughter's chase,
With jars of dreams, we find our place!

Breezes Carrying Laughter

The air is filled with jokes so loud,
As kids play tag, we watch them proud.
An ice cream truck approaches slow,
But guess what? My change fell in the snow!

Laughter echoes as we all dive,
Trying to survive a swarm alive.
A bee buzzes by—oh, what a surprise!
In terror, I scream, 'Will it eat my fries?'

The wind brings scents of grill and fun,
While dad flips burgers, thinking he's won.
A cloud of smoke, a charred delight,
Did we just burn the buns? Oh, what a sight!

As twilight fades, we all unwind,
With stories shared, our hearts combined.
The breezes carry laughter anew,
In every chuckle, love shines through!

A Collection of Little Things

Squeaky chairs and old routine,
A place for laughs, a sight unseen.
Dogs chase squirrels, a playful dance,
We sip our drinks and take a chance.

Sunsets spill like orange jam,
While neighbors yell for their pet lamb.
I spill my soda, you roll your eyes,
It's chaos here, but what a prize!

Mismatched socks on everyone's feet,
We laugh at names we'd never meet.
Fried chicken crumbs on the floor,
Who needs a beach? We've got this door!

Worn-out shoes and stories bold,
The warmth of laughter, as tales unfold.
In this little spot, we feel so free,
Home isn't just walls, it's you and me!

The Quiet Call of Familiar Spaces

A rusted swing set calls my name,
With every creak, it feels the same.
The smell of cookies from mom's hand,
Gingerbread dreams on sugary sand.

Neighbors gossip about the rain,
Umbrellas flip and folks complain.
But here we joke, it's quite a scene,
As we plot on how to stay unseen.

Ghosts of meetings come to play,
With old board games we've lost the way.
Your laugh is stuck in my brain,
Can someone please explain this gain?

Time flies on, yet here we sit,
Chasing moments, not a bit of wit.
With ice cream drips and joyous screams,
In this sweet chaos, we build our dreams!

Gathering Clouds of Nostalgia

Rainy days bring out the fun,
Puddle jumping, oh what a run!
Cats on laps and TV shows,
We trade our laughs and silly woes.

The toast is burnt, the coffee's cold,
But every mishap feels like gold.
Like jigsaw puzzles on the floor,
Together, we just want some more.

Whispers shared beneath the stars,
We log our tales in cookie jars.
The crickets chirp a silly tune,
As we question life, and eat through June.

With each old song, a familiar beat,
We dance around with silly feet.
In this eccentric, chaotic cheer,
We find our home, year after year!

Where Dreams Find Their Rest

In the corner, a cat naps wide,
Dreaming of fish and a lazy slide.
As squirrels plot their daring heists,
We laugh and munch on leftover bites.

Chairs creak with tales of wild nights,
With ice cream spills, and friendly fights.
Cousins jump up with a sudden sound,
While grandpa's snore rolls all around.

Sunlight dances, time lingers long,
With rubber bands fired, who can go wrong?
Shoes stacked like trophies from battles won,
Victory declared with each hapless run.

Even the wind seems to chuckle here,
Tugging at hats and stirring cheer.
Where squishy cushions hold secrets tight,
And laughter echoes into the night.

Pairs of Shoes Neatly Lined

On the mat, a pair of boots,
Beside them lie some silly hoots.
Flip-flops giggle, loafers sigh,
As sneaker chatter flits nearby.

Each step held tales in their tread,
Of jogs and jumps, and what was said.
Old sandals whisper of summer fun,
While heels recall a quickened run.

With every visit, a new cast arrives,
Sneaking stories, oh how it thrives!
Dancing shoes join the happy fleet,
In a messy line, far from discreet.

Unable to contain their playful pride,
They plot mischief with the yard wide.
As evening draws near and moonlight beams,
The shoes conspire, fueling dreams.

Echoes of Laughter Between the Walls

A knock, a friend, then all the cheer,
While echoes bounce from ear to ear.
Pillow fights and taco runs,
Life's sweetest moments, all in puns.

Old photos hang like trusty guides,
Winking tales where humor resides.
Each frame a riddle, a comic twist,
A spaghetti drop, oh what a list.

In these corners, shadows play tricks,
Hilarious falls, and slapstick kicks.
With every giggle, the twinkling lights,
Reflecting joys in silly fights.

What mischief brews behind closed doors?
Who knows what wacky time restores?
But here we gather, no worries, just glee,
Among the walls, wild and free.

The Silent Witness of Serenity

In the stillness, a squirrel prances,
Spinning tales of chance romances.
Light through leaves creates a dance,
While we wiggle, lost in the trance.

Mismatched cushions hold us tight,
As laughter blooms, pure delight.
Quiet whispers turned loud and bold,
In a space that hugs, all hearts unfold.

Lost in thoughts and silly dreams,
Our cozy nook is bursting at the seams.
With silly hats and fluffed-up hair,
The shyest amongst us dares to share.

Each echo cradles warmth and charm,
While breeze brings in another calm.
What is unseen becomes supreme,
In this haven where we dare to dream.

Sipping Sunshine and Sweetness

With lemonade in hand, I sit
The sun's a friend, and bugs a bit
A bird lands nearby, with a cheeky song
Even the squirrels agree, this spot's not wrong.

The neighbor's dog barks, it's quite a delight
He thinks he's a wolf, in a small city fight
A cat on the fence, gives a look of disdain
As if to say, 'what's all this fuss and gain?'

My chair creaks a tune, like a rusty old band
Supporting my laughter, and snacks at hand
With each silly joke, the hours slip away
These moments are treasures, come what may.

So raise your glass high, to this silly affair
With sunshine and sweetness, and love in the air
For laughter is bright, where the heart finds its place
In the joy of the everyday, life's a warm embrace.

Shadows Dance in Golden Rays

The sun dips low, shadows creep
As laughter rises, and worries sleep
A squirrel performs, on a tightrope of wires
Impressing the kids, igniting their fires.

The barbeque's smokin', my dad's on the grill
He's flipping the burgers, but it's all downhill
For when the smoke clears, he's made quite a mess
The hotdogs are dancing, I must confess!

This stage of sunshine, where laughter is king
With wild melodies, the evening does sing
An ice cream lady strolls by with a wink
As we all gather 'round, sharing jokes and a drink.

So here we shall stay, when the day shakes our hand
With shadows that twirl, in our own little band
For moments like this, are what dreams are made of
In the light-hearted space, we find what we love.

A Seat for the Soul's Rest

In my favorite chair, the world fades away
With a snack in my lap, and the sky blue and gray
Feet propped up high, I feel like a queen
As the cat plots mischief, a sight to be seen.

A drink spills with laughter, as friends call my name
We share all our stories, like each one's a game
The gossip's absurd, the punchlines are bold
Each tale overlapped, like stitches of gold.

Thunder rolls in, but we're safe and secure
As we brave all the storms, with laughter so pure
Through rain and through sun, our spirits align
In this cozy arena, life's downright divine.

So to all of you seekers, sit down, take a pause
For this little seat's magic deserves a round of applause
A sanctuary made, with each giggle and jest
In the heart of our gathering, we all find our rest.

Canvas of Life in Every Season

With paintbrush in hand, I'll capture today
Each color a giggle, in life's grand display
A dash of bright yellow, to lighten the mood
While the clouds of gray bring a laugh, not a brood.

Autumn's a painter, with pumpkins alive
While winter drops snow, making snowmen thrive
In spring, flowers bloom, a festival's cheer
And summer says 'hello' with warm, sunny beer.

Every season's a joke, that we all can embrace
A canvas of moments, in raucous grace
The colors swirl wildly, like laughter we trace
Life's art is a riot, a bright, loving space.

So join in the laughter, come add to my scheme
For life's but a canvas, don't miss out on the theme
With brushes of joy, let's create, let's unwind
In this whimsical painting, where warmth we all find.

Sunlit Sanctuary at Twilight

In the fading light, chairs creak and groan,
Cats chase shadows, making the place their own.
Lemonade spills, a moment of grace,
As we watch the sun slip, it's a funny race.

Grandma's tales, she weaves with flair,
About the time Dad got stuck in a chair.
Everyone giggles, the fireflies dance,
In this silly place, we all take a chance.

A dog rolls by, covered in mud,
Cousins have painted his belly a dud.
We howl with laughter, no plume of regret,
In our cozy bubble, we remain a duet.

As night gently falls, the stars appear bright,
We crack more jokes, oh what a sight!
In our little haven, with all the fun,
Twilight settles in, but the laughter's just begun.

Laughter Lingers in the Air

Swinging to and fro, the breeze brings cheer,
With each belly laugh, worries disappear.
Mom's burnt cookies, the mystery unfurls,
Frogs wearing chef hats and aprons twirl.

Sipping iced tea, a sudden bee buzz,
Dad swats with flair, like it's all just because.
Splat! On his forehead, it lands with a plop,
We laugh till we cry, and the silly won't stop.

Throwing popcorn, a playful brawl,
Uncle Bob ducks, but he's too big to fall.
Mice with tiny helmets conduct the show,
As giggles bounce, filling space like a glow.

Under string lights, we weave tales so wacky,
Here's to the folly, and never feeling tacky!
Laughter lingers, like sweet summer air,
In this cheerful refuge, we banter without care.

Beneath the Canopy of Stars

Peeking at the heavens, we search for a prize,
"Is that a comet?" a cousin theorizes.
Slipping off sandals, toes in the grass,
Fingers pointing out constellations that pass.

Uncle Joe insists he saw a UFO,
Made by his neighbor and powered by dough.
We giggle and snicker, as stories unfold,
About how the aliens like nachos and gold.

"Who brought the snacks?" a voice cries in horror,
Someone reveals a bag of marshmallow borer.
S'mores in process; chocolate's a must,
As laughter erupts and we sprinkle the dust.

A pile of blankets, we snuggle, we tease,
As the stars twinkle down, we feel the bliss breeze.
In this wild backyard, oh so far from the norm,
Silly giggles rise up—a most wonderful form.

A Glimpse of Everyday Bliss

On wicker chairs, we spin silly tales,
Of the time those squirrels tried stealing our snacks.
With overturned cups and giggles galore,
Each moment spins magic, we always want more.

A kettle whistles, a dance in the air,
Tea bags pirouette like they haven't a care.
Someone trips over a garden hose snake,
We laugh till our sides ache, it's all in good stakes.

Neighbors poke heads, "What happened, oh dear?"
They smile at our giggles, the warmth's drawing near.
With lemonade spilled, we roll on the floor,
In this little escape, we all want much more.

As twilight embraces, we sit in a line,
Sharing our stories, and passing the wine.
In this merry embrace, all were given a pass,
For every moment is funny, and nothing's too crass.

A Siesta of the Heart

Sunlight spills, a lazy beam,
Cat sprawled out, a fluffy dream.
Neighbors wave, dogs dig in mud,
Life's a breeze, while I'm a dud.

Lemonade in hand, I sigh,
A squirrel steals my slice of pie.
Laughter rings in the warm, sweet air,
Just another day without a care.

Chairs creak softly as I recline,
In this lazy land, I'm divine.
A nap calls me, oh, what a tease,
But who needs sleep when I've got cheese?

Time drifts slow like a snail on toast,
I wake from dreams, but I'm still a ghost.
Blissfully trapped in my comfy spot,
A siesta's charm, it hits the spot!

Alluring Gardens of Thought

Petunias bloom under the sun,
I wrestle weeds, who think it's fun.
A lawn gnome winks, what a surprise,
I swear its eyes outshine the skies.

Thoughts dance 'round like butterflies,
One lands here, it's wearing ties.
"Water me," it sweetly pleads,
I just ignore the tangled reeds.

Rabbits hop, causing a stir,
Stealing dreams, my gourmet burr.
In this wild plot, wisdom grows,
Right next to tomatoes; who knows?

Mismatched flowers, blooming with flair,
A daisies' debate with a cactus' glare.
In this garden, I chuckle and play,
Who knew we'd plant joy every day?

Paper Boats in Gentle Winds

Folded dreams float on a stream,
Laughter echoes, a happy theme.
Kids chase ducks, and giggles soar,
While I sit here, wanting more.

Wind kisses cheeks, it twirls a hat,
Splat! A bird drops a crumbly brat.
It sails away on a paper glide,
While I ponder, oh, where's my pride?

Clouds parade in a cotton-puff race,
Shadows dance, no time to waste.
With each gust, new stories to spin,
Like paper boats, let the fun begin!

By sun or storm, joy is my friend,
Every moment's a chance to bend.
In giggles and sails, lives intertwine,
Our paper dreams—oh, how divine!

Shadows Cast by Flickering Flames

Night falls soft like a cozy sweater,
Bugs buzz by; they sure know better.
Firelight flickers on faces bright,
Telling tales that dance in the night.

Marshmallows roast with a gentle thud,
In the laughter's warmth, we all feel snug.
A ghost story, oh what a joke,
The punchline's lost in the smoky smoke.

Shadows leap like they're playing tag,
While I fight hard not to brag.
About my skills with a stick and spark,
But hey, my marshmallows? Quite the mark!

Under stars, we find our place,
In the ember's glow, a silly race.
Who knew the magic of a flickering light,
Could twist and turn a snort into night?

Where Nature Meets Nurture

Beneath the shade of swaying trees,
The squirrels play hide and seek with bees.
My coffee spills, I laugh and frown,
As pigeons strut like they own this town.

A chair that creaks, it sings a tune,
While I contemplate the rising moon.
The garden gnomes, they wink and nod,
Surely they've seen the strangest facade.

Reflection and Reverie Unfold

The cat sprawls wide, like she owns the space,
While I try to find my usual place.
The cushions bounce as dreams take flight,
Here the world feels both snug and bright.

The wind chimes jangle, a curious song,
I ponder if I've been here too long.
Glancing at clouds that look like fluff,
I'm the king; life's perfect, enough is enough.

Ties That Bind in the Open Air

Neighbors argue over grass length,
As I sip tea, draining their strength.
Laughter spills over the fence's edge,
I promise it's better than jumping a hedge!

Dogs bark loudly, a real tough crew,
They plot mischief like only they do.
With the sun shining, hearts feel wide,
Invite a friend; let the fun coincide.

Heartstrings and Morning Glories

With morning glory twisting 'round,
Eccentric neighbors gather 'round.
They tell tall tales of their backyard quests,
I laugh so hard, I can barely rest.

Birds chirp gossip, a breezy jest,
As I lounge here, I feel so blessed.
Each moment shared, a memory made,
In this quirky world of sun and shade.

Breathe Deep in the Twilight

Sunset throws a wink my way,
As my cat claims my favorite chair.
Sipping tea, I start to sway,
Dreaming of fluffy clouds in air.

Neighbors chatting, laughter loud,
My dog joins in, barks so sweet.
Strangled jokes, they form a crowd,
Even ghosts would dance on their feet.

Cicadas sing their night-time tune,
While I swear the lamp's got a glow.
I pretend I'm a cartoon raccoon,
Raiding dishes while others don't know.

The stars are tipsy, swaying low,
In this mix of cheer and clatter.
Who needs a show, or a grandiose show?
With friends like these, it's all that matters.

Blessings in the Company of Stars

Under twinkling lights we share,
Secrets like candy from a jar.
One friend spills tea; we sigh, 'Who cares?'
We laugh as if we've traveled far.

The moon's a witness to our plots,
Conspiracy theories on a roll.
Everyone thinks we're simply knots,
But we're stargazers with a goal.

Frogs join in with their croaky lines,
As we debate life's great conundrums.
Should we get tacos or fish tacos?
We laugh, because, truly, why choose just one?

With each sip, our dreams take flight,
Like balloons escaping from a hand.
We'll solve it all with love tonight,
And maybe even start a band.

Time's Gentle Hand on the Heart

The clock ticks funny, out of tune,
As I search for my other sock.
Laughter dances – how cute, how June!,
And my mind's stuck on the last TikTok.

Bingo nights turn into wild games,
Of charades and hula-hooping fits.
Old folks grab their canes, call names,
As I fall trying to show off my splits.

Time's a slippery little eel,
Where does it go when I can't see?
It giggles, too; it feels surreal,
I trip over what used to be free.

In the end, we all end up old,
But we'll still be young at the heart.
With stories funny and memories bold,
In this game of life, we each play our part.

Warm Moods and Winter Nights

Snow lays soft on ground and minds,
As cocoa warms our chilly tips.
Socks misplace in all the finds,
And laughter spills from happy lips.

Blankets piled like joyful forts,
We're kingdom builders, if just for fun.
Sledding down with silly shouts,
Soon we'll say, 'How can winter run?'

The fireplace flickers, shadows play,
Telling tales of mischief past.
Hot dogs roasted in a display,
As winter kisses us, and laughs amassed.

Now, with cheeks bright and spirits high,
We toast with marshmallows on a chance,
In this cozy space, we'll fly,
Letting winter weave our laughter's dance.

Embraced by Nature's Breath

Breezes whisper jokes to trees,
As squirrels giggle with delight.
A rocking chair creaks with ease,
While critters join the late-night flight.

The cat debates with stars above,
A dog barks at the moon's strange glow.
Fireflies blink in rhythmic love,
As laughter dances to and fro.

The world slows down, the sun bids adieu,
A mischief-maker hangs from a vine.
Nature's laughter brings joy anew,
Each moment feels just so divine.

Underneath this leafy dome,
We sip our drinks and share a tale.
Here we find our hearts a-home,
In nature's winks, we shall prevail.

The Heartbeat of the Evening

The blame's on the crickets' chirpy song,
For making everyone dance a groove.
They think we dance the whole night long,
But we just sway, ain't got no move.

The wind's a comedian, with jokes in tow,
Tickling the leaves until they flutter.
A fence post laughs at a stray cat's show,
As shadows mingle, we can't help but mutter.

Moths throwing parties, so wild and free,
While the porch light serves as their ball.
Underneath all this laughter, you see,
We forget the world, lost in it all.

Neighbors peek in with grins so wide,
Their laughter parts the evening's mist.
In this shared joy, we all abide,
As the stars play hide and seek with our tryst.

Dancing Shadows on the Floor

Here the shadows stretch and play,
Chasing each other all around.
They twist and twirl, what a display,
As laughter's echoes swirl and sound.

The moon, a spotlight on our stage,
With fireflies as backup flair.
A misstep leads to giggles, sage,
As we all flop with style and care.

The night has no dull moments here,
Sipping sweet tea, our secret blend.
Each stumble's met with hearty cheer,
As shadows dance, and we pretend.

With every chuckle, hearts expand,
In this spectacle of night's delight.
We're just a bunch with mischief planned,
Creating memories, bold and bright.

Stories of Old and Dreams Yet to Be

Gather round for tales so bold,
Of socks mismatched and shoes untied.
These stories gather like fine gold,
As laughter brims and fears are dried.

A grandpa's yarn of a cat that swam,
Who chased a fish on a dare, oh my!
Each twist and turn, he's such a ham,
We belly-laugh as hours go by.

With dreams that leap like frogs in spring,
Our minds take flight on whispering winds.
In this circle, our hearts all sing,
As we weave what our spirit intends.

So here we sit, with memories tight,
In this joyful haze, all things align.
Under stars that twinkle at night,
Life is a joke, and we're doing fine.

Whispers of Dusk and Dawn

As the sun bids goodbye with a wink,
I ponder if bugs have time to think.
The cat leaps high, but lands in mud,
While I just giggle, a real-life dud.

Stars twinkle like they're playing tricks,
While I question my snack choices, guilty of fix.
A breeze whispers secrets, I stare in delight,
As the raccoon waltzes and gives me a fright.

The laugh of a child fills the air,
As grandma's voice yells, "Don't you dare!"
Above, the moon chuckles softly at me,
Was that really a shadow, or just a spilled tea?

Fireflies dance, making sparks of night,
While my dog chases them with all his might.
I sip lemonade, thoughtful with glee,
In this goofy kingdom, the ruler is me.

A Seat Between Shadows

Nestled between whispers of light and shade,
I ponder why squirrels try to evade.
The garden hose spritzes, a sudden surprise,
While I dodge, laughing at garden spies.

Bouncing chairs with their creaks and moans,
Make me feel like our house has grown bones.
A neighbor's dog spots me, gives a bark,
And I wonder, does he think I'm a lark?

The wind tickles my nose, oh what a prank!
While I contemplate if it's time for a tank.
My thoughts flutter like butterflies in flight,
And I giggle at shadows that startle the night.

Clouds play hide and seek, dressed like sheep,
While laughter escapes as my thoughts start to leap.
With each silly act of the trees and the light,
This quirky hideaway feels perfectly right.

Where the Evening Breathes

The sun yawns wide, stretching over the leaves,
As I sip my drink filled with curious peaves.
Jokes amongst crickets buzz by, full-blown,
While a moth twirls like it's never alone.

A squirrel drops an acorn, what a sight,
The cat snickers, thinking he's witty and bright.
Neighbors exchange tales, and giggles ensue,
While I contemplate if I need one more brew.

Laughter fills the air, it's a quirky tune,
As the fireflies gather, cueing the moon.
And somewhere a coyote's howling refrain,
Makes us laugh harder and raise our disdain.

With each passing hour, the sky turns to navy,
As a child's toy falls, it's definitely wavy.
Here in this humor where laughter evokes,
Even sweaty summers turn into gentle jokes.

Embrace of the Gentle Breeze

In the gentle hug of the nighttime air,
I ponder if birds have time to care.
With a swoop and a dive, their antics amuse,
While ants carry crumbs, forming their crews.

A chair whines under my weight, oh dear,
Can it take my squirming? I hope it won't leer!
At twilight's canvass, colors collide,
As I toss snacks to the dog by my side.

The neighborhood laughter spills like wine,
While I chat with the grass, it's green and divine.
A frog croaks his story, bold and loud,
As if he's the king, proud in the crowd.

The stars blink down, sharing their jest,
While I muse on the day, feeling truly blessed.
Amid all this nonsense, life gives a cheer,
In this cozy realm, I've no guilt, just cheer.

Footprints on the Threshold

Beneath the old swing, dust bunnies dance,
My cat plots mischief, caught in a trance.
Neighbors glance over, with curious eyes,
Wondering how I survive all these pies.

Flip-flops are scattered, a colorful mess,
I trip on the mat, but who would guess?
Laughter erupts as I tumble and roll,
Mom's secret recipe stuffed in my bowl.

Sunshine spills in, the day's getting bright,
Gossip with squirrels makes everything right.
Birds chirp their gossip, they're quite the crew,
My audience here, they're a feathery view.

A lazy dog snorts, dreams of chasing the mail,
He'd pounce on that letter, sure without fail.
With warmth on my face, this chaos feels fine,
Let the world spin fast; here, I just shine.

Time's Gentle Embrace

A rocking chair squeaks like a mischievous tease,
As I sip iced tea, feeling just like a breeze.
Old Timmy the turtle thinks he's quite quick,
While he races the breeze, I know he won't stick.

The sun dips low, casting shadows so long,
I burst into song, though my notes are quite wrong.
Confetti of leaves twirls down from above,
Nature seems to giggle, oh, how it does love!

The mailman walks by in his bright-yellow suit,
I shout out a greeting, he's one silly hoot!
Terracotta pots filled with flowers so wild,
Paint a picture of joy, whimsical and styled.

Time here suspends, like a bubble in air,
Where laughter and warmth blend into a prayer.
Settle with me, let the world's hustle go,
In this spot of bliss, we'll nibble on woe.

Where Solitude Meets Serenity

A chair without cushions, yet never feels bare,
I sit and I ponder, without a care.
Insects hum softly, an off-key duet,
Nature's orchestra, a favorite set!

A frog croaks a tale of romance and strife,
While fireflies wink, sparkling with life.
An empty glass sits, it's time for a refill,
As I laugh with the breeze, my heart feels the thrill.

Mismatched socks hang from the sunniest line,
A tribute to chaos, of life pure divine.
Coffee's my muse as the world fades away,
Here's to life's madness, come join in the play!

In solitude's arms, I find my delight,
Unwrapped in the wonder, it feels just right.
So let laughter echo, let joy take the lead,
In this space of my choosing, I plant every seed.

A Safe Harbor at Dusk

As the sun dips low, the cat leaps up high,
While I ponder a snack and a soft, gentle sigh.
The old porch squeaks like a friendly old ghost,
Sharing its secrets like a fond, silly boast.

Fireflies flicker, a disco so bright,
While crickets debate who can sing through the night.
A juggling of bugs in midair's the show,
As I sip from my cup, oh, the laughter will flow!

A cushion's my throne in this rustic retreat,
While shoes scatter tales of adventure so sweet.
With each passing second, the chaos makes sense,
We'll dance with the shadows, a glorious immense!

Dusk wraps around like a favorite blanket,
Whispers of daylight keep flitting to bank it.
With a chuckle and smile, let mischief arise,
In this twilight harbor, all worries disguise.

The Warmth of Private Corners

In a chair that squeaks and moans,
I sit and chat with my plant's old bones.
The cat thinks he runs the show,
But really, he just steals my toe!

A neighbor yells about their trash,
While I sip tea, trying not to splash.
The garden gnomes plot a scheme,
To steal my snacks in the sunbeam!

Birds chirp gossip from a tree,
Of their secret flight to the local flea.
I join their chatter, just for fun,
But they say I'm just a silly one!

Laughter dances in the air,
As I spin tales without a care.
Every moment feels quite grand,
In my corner, life's so unplanned!

Gathering Tales at Day's End

Sunset brings a golden glow,
And my dog thinks he's the pro.
He hiccups after his treats,
While I ponder life's odd beats!

Old friends drop by with their quirks,
Telling stories with silly smirks.
The fire crackles with delight,
As we roast marshmallows, what a sight!

A raccoon joins the fun, it seems,
Searching for snacks, chasing dreams.
We giggle at his sneaky ways,
As dusk turns into silly plays!

With laughter ringing in the air,
We share our woes, but mostly care.
As night unfolds its starry shawl,
We cling to memories, most of all!

The Symphony of Nature's Heart

The wind whistles a funny tune,
While bugs dance beneath the moon.
Crickets chirp a silly song,
As I hum along, not knowing wrong!

A squirrel steals my peanut stash,
With a furious dash, oh what a clash!
He thinks he's won the comedy war,
But I'll unleash my secret encore!

The trees gossip with a creak,
Whispering jokes, unique and sleek.
I laugh along with the stars' bright glow,
In this silly world, I feel the flow!

Nature's heart beats with a grin,
As laughter spills from deep within.
Every leaves' rustle calls my name,
In this symphony, I join the game!

A Canvas of Quiet Reflection

With crayons drawn in nature's light,
I doodle dreams, oh what a sight!
The butterflies giggle, flitting by,
As I draw a cat that can fly!

Raindrops tap on my rusty roof,
While I sip coffee, chasing goof.
A splash of paint, a splash of grace,
This quiet scene, a funny space!

Chasing shadows, playing tag,
While ducks waddle with a brag.
I paint their quirks with each quick stroke,
Creating tales that make me choke!

With each brush, a story grows,
In this corner where laughter flows.
Reflections blur in colors bright,
As I embrace this funny night!

Simple Pleasures of the Unseen

On my steps, the dog snores loud,
With tail wagging, he's so proud.
The cat plots out her daily schemes,
While I sip tea and chase my dreams.

Neighbors gossip, in whispers low,
Over fences, secrets flow.
I watch them argue, just for fun,
While counting clouds, I lose the sun.

Squirrels steal the birdseed stash,
While the goldfish does a splash.
My shoes misplaced, a funny sight,
I wore them backwards—oh, what a fright!

Breezy chill, the evening's nigh,
I give a laugh, and wonder why.
With each chuckle, the world feels right,
In this haven, my heart's delight.

Comfort Crafted in Humble Wood

Old rocking chair creaks like it's alive,
Each squeak and sway brings joy to thrive.
My coffee's cold, but that's quite fine,
It's just a reason to sip some wine.

A pile of shoes, all mixed and matched,
When did I wear those? I'm not quite hatched.
The garden gnome looks quite absurd,
But he just laughs, not saying a word.

Random bugs host a nightly show,
As I watch them dance, just taking it slow.
Mismatched socks, a curious plight,
I sport them proudly, much to my delight!

Crickets chirp a tune so sweet,
While I kick back, embracing defeat.
In this chaos, my spirit soars,
Within this mess, my heart restores.

Whispers in the Twilight

The twilight air hums with delight,
As fireflies put on a glowing fight.
Bugs colliding—oh! What a scene,
Like tiny dancers, they're oh-so-keen.

A chair reclines with style unmatched,
I tumble back and find I'm hatched.
A wayward cat, in moonlight found,
Flops on my lap, with a graceful bound.

Did I mention the pie I baked?
It's half-gone now, and tastefully faked.
Neighbors stand peeking, curious eyes,
"Where's the rest?" they tease, to my surprise!

The stars giggle, they wink and gleam,
As I dream up my chaotic scheme.
In these moments of silly bliss,
I wonder how I could ever miss.

Embracing the Evening Breeze

Evening breezes tickle my face,
As chairs serenade with gentle grace.
A wind chime's song is out of tune,
But I join in, an off-key croon.

A spider spins her web with flair,
While I untangle my own hair.
A game of tag with shadows plays,
As laughter mingles with sun's last rays.

Who needs a movie when you've got this?
Nature's comedy brings pure bliss.
An army of ants march with pride,
Stealing crumbs I thought I'd hide.

As daylight fades, the world's aglow,
With friends nearby, we'd steal the show.
In this laughter, my spirit flies,
Underneath the starlit skies.

Musings in the Sunlight

Sitting on the steps, I ponder and grin,
A squirrel scurries by, with a nut for a win.
The world rushes past, but here, I just stay,
In my throne of old wood, the sun's on full play.

Neighbors walk by with their curious stares,
As I lounge in my slippers, dodging their glares.
A bird sings a tune, but he's off-key, oh dear,
Yet his notes bring me joy, and I start to cheer.

The mailman arrives, with a wink and a wave,
Delivering bills that I'll never behave.
But laughter erupts as I dodge his quick smile,
Pretending I'm busy, oh, what a fine style!

Butterflies dance like they own the whole scene,
While I'm sipping my lemonade, feeling so keen.
Life's simple here, amidst laughter and light,
This spot's my escape; it makes everything right.

Sipping Tea Under the Sky

Tea's brewing nicely, with flavors galore,
I spill it on my lap—oh, I'll need to pour more.
With friends all around, they're laughing out loud,
The cat's in my lap, and he's feeling so proud.

Gossiping softly, our secrets take flight,
As the wind blows through hair, causing sheer delight.
Oh, who spilled the beans on who dated who first?
Our tales sway like branches, and laughter unburst.

The sun starts to set, painting skies with a brush,
While we raise our mugs, in a jovial hush.
The dog joins the fun with his goofy little dance,
He trips on the rug; we assume it's romance!

A melon-sized bee thinks he's joining the crew,
Buzzing by my head like he's got some joke too.
Yet we sip in good spirits, no worries tonight,
For every wild moment makes everything right.

Memories in the Rustle of Leaves

Leaves crunch beneath feet, like the snacks I adore,
As I chase my old memories, behind the front door.
The kids ride their bikes, oh, what a delight,
While I grab my old chair, and settle in tight.

A game of tag starts, with laughter so loud,
But soon someone trips, oh, I'm lost in that crowd.
With a snack in my pocket, I watch them all play,
Feeling wiser than ever, in my comfy array.

The dog brings me a stick, like it's treasure found,
I throw it away; oh, he's racing around!
I'm the queen of this kingdom, snug as a bug,
As everyone stops for a quick, cheerful hug.

The golden sun fades, and it tickles my face,
As twilight whispers softly, like an old friend's embrace.
I sigh with a smile—what a marvelous day,
These moments are magic, come what may.

A Retreat from the Outside World

In my little corner, where chaos won't tread,
I escape from the noise with my biscuits and bread.
The neighbors grill burgers while I make my peace,
Finding joy in the silence, my quirky release.

Lawn chairs are set, in a very odd way,
With a wind chime that sings, come what may.
Children run wild; they're hunting for bugs,
While I nap in the shade, like a wise, lazy slug.

Talk of the town drifts, like leaves in the breeze,
But I sip my cold drink, and do just as I please.
The bugs play their symphony, loud and off-key,
Yet I love every note, in each perfect decree.

As dusk starts to fall, and the stars peek on through,
I take one last bite of that pie; it's a view!
With laughter and snacks, this spot feels so right,
In this haven of giggles, I'll stay here tonight.

Threads of Connection Unraveled

A cat on a cushion, regal and grand,
It snores so loudly, you'd think it could stand.
Grandma's old tales, with laughter laced tight,
Like socks in the dryer, they vanish from sight.

Uncle Joe's jokes, they rarely land well,
He laughs at his punchlines; it's harder to tell.
With chips scattered wide and drinks overflowing,
We're all tightly woven, even when throwing.

Neighbors peeking in, they're curious folk,
We wave and we chuckle, a shared little joke.
In a world of connections, both tangled and neat,
We treasure the moments that make us feel sweet.

So come join the chaos and dance with delight,
Life's threads may unravel, but oh, what a sight!
In this motley crew, where misfits align,
You'll find joy in laughter, in every weird sign.

Autumn Leaves in Quiet Confession

The leaves fall like gossip, a vibrant cascade,
Whispers of autumn, in colors displayed.
A squirrel with a stash, thinks he's won the game,
While we shrug and chuckle, a whole park's his claim.

Hot cider's a treasure, with spices that dance,
But every time I sip, I spill—what a chance!
I'm saving it all for that perfect cold day,
Yet every warm gulp feels like summer's bouquet.

So check your pockets; it's where all the crumbs,
From snacks shared in joy turn to trails of hums.
We gather like leaves, in a swirling embrace,
Each laugh like a twirl, in this whimsical space.

With pumpkins a-grinning, we can't help but gloat,
And here's to the fun, as we bumble and float.
Our little confessions, this laughter, this cheer,
Are all tied together, by the season so dear.

The Essence of Togetherness

We gather like pigeons, in a huddle of mirth,
Sharing our stories, in all we're worth.
A chicken leg's battle, who's winning today?
With laughter erupting, the winner gives way.

The weather is fickle, yet we're sun-soaked in fun,
Arguing who's fastest but guessing who's won.
We're poets of chaos, in our curious ways,
Each muffin a masterpiece, in buttered displays.

An impromptu dance-off breaks out with a grin,
As Aunt Mabel twirls, we all rush to join in.
Her moves are a riot, her laughter contagious,
This essence of joy is simply outrageous.

With hearts intertwined, and snacks in a pile,
Each goofy endeavor is met with a smile.
In the garden of chaos, where humor's the plant,
We cultivate moments, and oh, how we chant!

Smiles Shared in Stillness

On a swing that creaks, we share quiet time,
Tickles of laughter, they bubble and rhyme.
The dog's tossed a stick, it's a game we all know,
Chasing our shadows, just letting it flow.

Birds lend their voices, a chorus of cheer,
As secrets are whispered, for only us here.
Grandpa's wise nod, he grades all our schemes,
While we plot our adventures, chasing our dreams.

A soft breeze descends, carrying laughter so light,
In moments of stillness, we feel pure delight.
We sip on sweet lemonade, it drips down our chins,
Winning the summer, where forever begins.

So catch these small moments, they shimmer and gleam,
In the tapestry of laughter, we stitch and we beam.
With smiles shared softly, and stories untold,
We gather our memories, precious as gold.

www.ingramcontent.com/pod-product-compliance
Lightning Source LLC
Chambersburg PA
CBHW062111280426
43661CB00086B/471